1

The
CLEAR and SIMPLE
Workbooks

Let's Sound Out Words

Grade 1
Phonics

By Nancy Jolson Leber & Liane B. Onish

Grosset & Dunlap

Cover Design by Traci Levine

Interior Design by Susan LiCalsi Design

Cover and Interior Illustrations by Bob Ostrom

GROSSET & DUNLAP

Published by the Penguin Group

Penguin Group (USA) Inc., 375 Hudson Street, New York, New York 10014, U.S.A.

Penguin Group (Canada), 90 Eglinton Avenue East, Suite 700, Toronto, Ontario, Canada M4P 2Y3
(a division of Pearson Penguin Canada Inc.)

Penguin Books Ltd, 80 Strand, London WC2R 0RL, England

Penguin Ireland, 25 St Stephen's Green, Dublin 2, Ireland
(a division of Penguin Books Ltd)

Penguin Group (Australia), 250 Camberwell Road, Camberwell, Victoria 3124, Australia
(a division of Pearson Australia Group Pty Ltd)

Penguin Books India Pvt Ltd, 11 Community Centre, Panchsheel Park, New Delhi - 110 017, India

Penguin Group (NZ), Cnr Airborne and Rosedale Roads, Albany, Auckland 1310, New Zealand
(a division of Pearson New Zealand Ltd)

Penguin Books (South Africa) (Pty) Ltd, 24 Sturdee Avenue, Rosebank, Johannesburg 2196, South Africa

Penguin Books Ltd, Registered Offices:
80 Strand, London WC2R 0RL, England

ISBN 0-448-44126-8   10 9 8 7 6 5 4 3 2 1

Dear Parents,

Clear and Simple Workbooks are designed to support you in guiding your emerging reader. Reading is essential to academic success. About 70 to 80 percent of children are able to break the sound/letter code after one year of instruction. Your first-grader can get ready by practicing the sounds that letters stand for (phonics), as well as learning sight words that do not follow regular spelling patterns and, therefore, cannot be sounded out.

Did you know?

- **Explicit, systematic phonics instruction is a successful way to teach young or slow-to-learn readers.**

- **Seeing a word while simultaneously hearing or saying it helps to spell it. Activities that focus on the structure of words help create visual images, which children will then use as they read and write. Self-correction is the single greatest factor in learning to spell.**

- **One-third of all our writing in English is made up of just 31 words! Learning to automatically recognize these words is critical for reading fluency.**

The skills needed for reading are complex, but Clear and Simple Workbooks make these skills . . . clear and simple. Each page introduces a phonics skill and a key picture, or a high-frequency word with reading and writing practice. Clear and Simple Workbooks make learning fun and easy for your child. Here's how:

- The simple, consistent design and the repetitive, patterned activities are predictable enough so that your child can use the books independently. In *Let's Sound Out Words*, your child will learn sound/letter relationships. In *I Can Read!*, your child will trace, read, and write new words and will then discriminate among different words and practice writing. Before long, your child will be able to identify direction words, such as *circle* and *color*.

- Clear and Simple Workbooks reinforce the new skills your child practices by providing storybooks in which words are repeated in a context your child can relate to.

- Some activities are open-ended, allowing for multiple correct answers as children work at their own level and feel successful. Furthermore, the review storybooks allow for creativity as your child will finish writing a page and illustrating it.

- Use Clear and Simple Workbooks as an opportunity for you and your child to spend quality time together. Have your child explain the pages to you and discuss the pictures. Get started by reading the first couple of pages aloud and working together. Provide crayons and pencils, along with a lot of support and praise.

Reading is the most important academic skill your child will learn. Make reading a positive, playful family experience using the Clear and Simple Workbook series.

Happy reading,

Nancy Jolson Leber

Nancy Jolson Leber
Educational Consultant

Liane B. Onish

Liane B. Onish
Educational Consultant

Consonant Review

B b C c D d F f

✏️ Trace the letters.

Match the pictures to the letters.

✏️ Color the pictures.

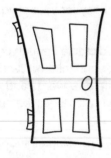 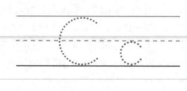 

 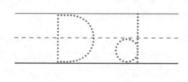 

 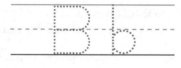 

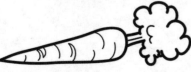  

Skill: Review Consonants /b/b, /k/c, /d/d, /f/f

G g  H h J j K k

✏️ Trace the letters.

Match the pictures to the letters.

🖍️ Color the pictures.

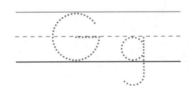

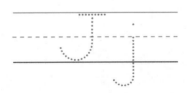

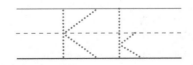

Skill: Review Consonants /g/g, /h/h, /j/j, /k/k

Consonant Review

L l   M m   N n   P p

✏️ Trace the letters.

Match the pictures to the letters.

🖍️ Color the pictures.

L l

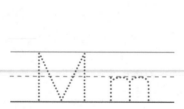
M m

N n

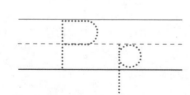

Skill: Review Consonants /l/ l, /m/ m, /n/ n, /p/ p

Q q R r S s T t

✏️ Trace the letters.

Match the pictures to the letters.

🖍️ Color the pictures.

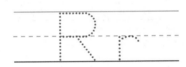

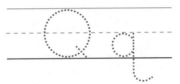

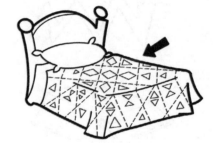

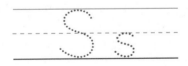

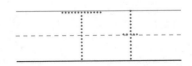

Skill: Review Consonants /kw/q, /r/r, /s/s, /t/t

Consonant Review

✏️ Trace the letters.

Match the pictures to the letters.

🖍️ Color the pictures.

Skill: Review Consonants /v/v, /w/w, /ks/x, /y/y, /z/z

Short Vowel a

 cat

Name what you see in the picture.

🖊 (Circle) the things with the short a sound as in cat.

Read the sentence.

🖊 Trace the letters that stand for the missing sounds.

Jack and Dad can cook.

Skill: Short Vowel /a/a

Jack has a cat.

✏️ Color the pictures.

✏️ Write a below each picture with the same short vowel sound as Jack.

 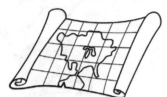  

_____   _____   _____   _____

‑‑a‑‑   ‑‑‑‑‑‑   ‑‑‑‑‑‑   ‑‑‑‑‑‑

✏️ Write the missing letter. Read the word.

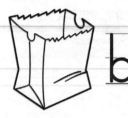 b ___ g    m ___ n    c ___ b

✏️ Write the word.

_____   _____   _____

Skill: Short Vowel /a/a

I Can

I can bat.

Directions: Help your child tear out this page and the next.
Staple along the cut edge. Have your child read the mini book.

I can tap.

I can wag.

I can _____

_____ .

Directions: Have your child draw a picture and complete the sentence.

Short Vowel i

 fish

Name what you see in the picture.

 Circle the things with the short i sound as in fish.

Read the sentence.

Trace the letters that stand for the missing sounds.

Min can swim.

Skill: Short Vowel /i/i

Min can fish.

🖍️ Color the pictures.

✏️ Write i below each picture with the same short vowel sound as Min.

_____   _____   _____   _____
- - - - - - - - - -   - - - - - - - - - -   - - - - - - - - - -   - - - - - - - - - -

✏️ Write the missing letter. Read the word.

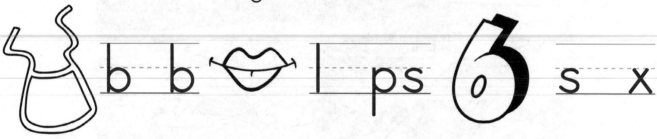

🖍️ Write the word.

_____   _____   _____
- - - - - - - - - -   - - - - - - - - - -   - - - - - - - - - -

HOME

Skill: Short Vowel /i/i

Short Vowel o

 lock

Name what you see in the picture.

 (Circle) the things with the short o sound as in lock.

Read the sentence.

 Trace the letters that stand for the missing sounds.

Rob can hop.

Skill: Short Vowel /o/o

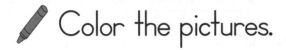 Rob can lock the box.

✏️ Color the pictures.

✏️ Write o below each picture with the same short vowel sound as Rob.

o _____   _____   _____   _____

✏️ Write the missing letter. Read the word.

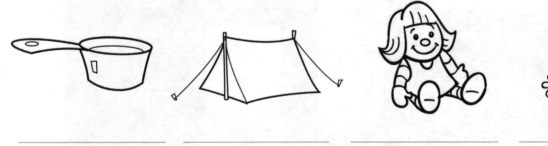

c _ b   r _ ck   b _ x

✏️ Write the word.

_____   _____   _____

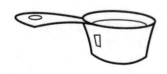

Short Vowel u

 cup

Name what you see in the picture.

 (Circle) the things with the short u sound as in cup.

Read the sentence.

 Trace the letters that stand for the missing sounds.

Bud can run.

Skill: Short Vowel /u/u

Bud can hug.

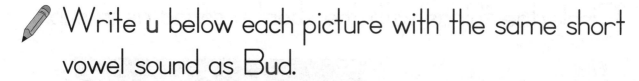

✏️ Color the pictures.

✏️ Write **u** below each picture with the same short vowel sound as Bud.

_____ _____ _____ _____
u

✏️ Write the missing letter. Read the word.

n _ t   b _ g   t _ b

✏️ Write the word.

_____ _____ _____

Short Vowel e

 bed

Name what you see in the picture.

Circle the things with the short e sound as in bed.

Read the sentence.

Trace the letters that stand for the missing sounds.

Jen can help.

Skill: Short Vowel /e/e

Jen can get in bed.

 Color the pictures.

✎ Write **e** below each picture with the same short vowel sound as Jen.

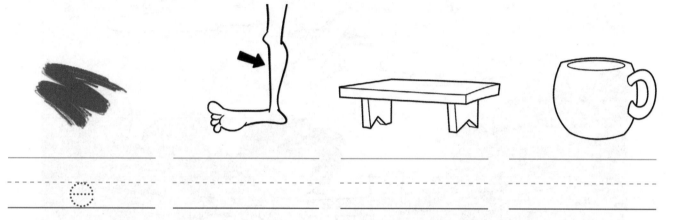

✎ Write the missing letter. Read the word.

p _ n   n _ st   b _ ll

✎ Write the word.

 HOME

Skill: Short Vowel /e/e

You Can

You can swim.

HOME

Directions: Help your child tear out this page and the next.
Staple along the cut edge. Have your child read the mini book.

You can beg.

You can hop.

You can run.

I can _____ .

Directions: Have your child draw a picture and complete the sentence.

Long Vowel a

 cake

Name what you see in the picture.

 Circle the things with the long a sound as in cake.

Read the sentences.

 Trace the letters that stand for the missing sounds.

Kate can skate.

She can wave to Jake.

Skill: Long Vowel /ā/ spelled a_e

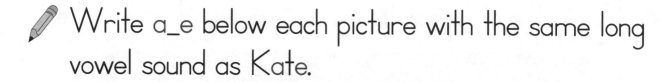

✎ Color the pictures.

✎ Write a_e below each picture with the same long vowel sound as Kate.

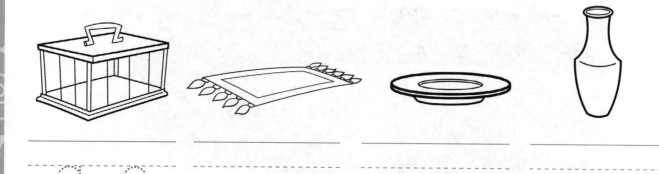

‑ ‑ ‑ a ‑ ‑ e ‑

✎ Write the missing letters. Read the word.

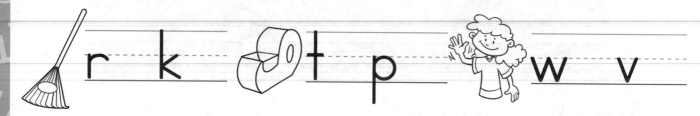

r k   t p   w v

✎ Write the word.

28   Skill: Long Vowel /ā/ spelled a_e

Long Vowel o

 rope

Name what you see in the picture.

 (Circle) the things with the long o sound as in rope.

Read the sentence.

 Trace the letters that stand for the missing sounds.

Hope can tell a joke.

Skill: Long Vowel /ō/ spelled o_e

Hope can jump rope.

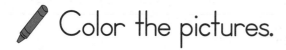

✏️ Color the pictures.

✏️ Write o_e below each picture with the same long vowel sound as Hope.

o _ e

✏️ Write the missing letters. Read the word.

 r b  h s p l

✏️ Write the word.

Skill: Long Vowel /ō/ spelled o_e

Long Vowel i

 bike

Name what you see in the picture.

 Circle the things with the long i sound as in bike.

Read the sentences.

 Trace the letters that stand for the missing sounds.

Mike can hike.

Then Mike can bike.

Skill: Long Vowel /ī/ spelled i_e

31

Mike likes his bike.

 Color the pictures.

 Write i_e below each picture with the same long vowel sound as Mike.

_____ _____ _____ _____

i _ e

 Write the missing letters. Read the word.

 c _____ 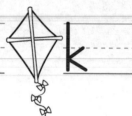 k t _____   m c

 Write the word.

_____ _____ _____

  Skill: Long Vowel /ī/ spelled i_e

We Can

Kate and I can skate.

Directions: Help your child tear out this page and the next.
Staple along the cut edge. Have your child read the mini book.

Mike and I can bike.

Jove can dig up a bone.

 We can _____ .

Directions: Have your child draw a picture and complete the sentence.

Long Vowel e

 feet

Name what you see in the picture.

 Circle the things with the long e sound
as in feet and Lee.

Read the sentence.

 Trace the letters that stand for the missing sounds.

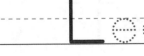 Lee can sweep.

Skill: Long Vowel /ē/ spelled ee

Long Vowel e

 leaf

Name what you see in the picture.

 Circle the things with the long e sound as in leaf and Jean.

Read the sentence.

 Trace the letters that stand for the missing sounds.

Jean can leap in the leaves.

 Skill: Long Vowel /ē/ spelled ea

Long Vowel a

 paint

Name what you see in the picture.

 Circle the things with the long a sound as in paint and Gail.

Read the sentence.

 Trace the letters that stand for the missing sounds.

Gail can e-mail.

Skill: Long Vowel /ā/spelled ai

Long Vowel a

 tray

Name what you see in the picture.

 Circle the things with the long a sound as in tray and Ray.

Read the sentence.

 Trace the letters that stand for the missing sounds.

Ray can play with clay.

Skill: Long Vowel /ā/ spelled ay

Long Vowel o

 roll

Name what you see in the picture.

 (Circle) the things with the long o sound
as in Bo and roll.

Read the sentence.

 Trace the letters that stand for the missing sounds.

Bo can hold the rolls.

Skill: Long Vowel /ō/ spelled o

Long Vowel o

 boat

Name what you see in the picture.

 Circle the things with the long o sound as in boat and Joan.

Read the sentence.

 Trace the letters that stand for the missing sounds.

Joan can feed a goat.

Skill: Long Vowel /ō/ spelled oa

Long Vowel i

 cry

Name what you see in the picture.

 Circle the things with the long i sound as in cry and Ty.

Read the sentence.

 Trace the letters that stand for the missing sounds.

Ty can dry.

Skill: Long Vowel /ī/ spelled y

Long Vowel i

 child

Name what you see in the picture.

 Circle the things with the long i sound as in child and Dinah.

Read the sentence.

Trace the letters that stand for the missing sounds.

Dinah can climb up high.

HOME

Skill: Long Vowel /ī/ spelled i

She Can! He Can!

Jean and Lee can eat green beans.

Directions: Help your child tear out this page and the next. Staple along the cut edge. Have your child read the mini book.

Gail and Ray can paint
it gray.

Joan and Bo can go
in a boat.

I can try _____.

 HOME

Directions: Have your child draw a picture and complete the sentence.

r-Blends br, pr, tr

 Write the letters that stand for the first sounds in each word.

_ _ br _ _ _ _ _ _ _ _ pr _ _ _ _ _ _ _ tr _ _ _ _

_____

- - - - - - - -

Read the sentences.

 (Circle) the letters that stand for the blends.

1. Princess Pru has a crown.

2. Brad brushes his hair.

3. Tracey has a toy train.

Skill: r-Blends

More r-Blends dr, fr, gr

 Write the letters that stand for the first sounds in each word.

dr _____   fr _____   gr _____

_____   _____   _____

_____   _____   _____

Read the sentences.

 (Circle) the letters that stand for the blends.

1. Drake paints a dragon.

2. Grace paints green grapes.

3. Frank paints a frog.

Skill: r-Blends

l-Blends gl, pl, sl

 Write the letters that stand for the first sounds in each word.

g   p   s

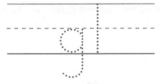

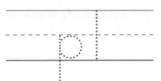

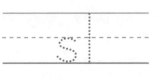

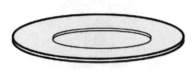

Read the sentences.

Circle the letters that stand for the blends.

1. Glen glides.

2. Placido plays.

3. Slade slides.

Skill: l-Blends

More l-Blends bl, cl, fl

✏️ Write the letters that stand for the first sounds in each word.

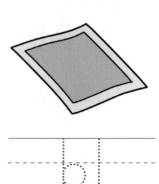

bl   cl   fl

Read the sentences.

✏️ Circle the letters that stand for the blends.

1. Blake blows bubbles.

2. Clark claps for the clown.

3. Flo plays the flute.

Skill: l-Blends

s-Blends sk, sn, sp

 Write the letters that stand for the first sounds in each word.

_____ sk _____   _____ sn _____   _____ sp _____

_____   _____   _____

_ _ _ _ _ _   _ _ _ _ _ _   _ _ _ _ _ _

_____   _____   _____

Read the sentences.

 (Circle) the letters that stand for the blends.

1. Skyler skips.

2. Spin spells.

3. Snap barks at a snake.

 Skill: s-Blends

More s-Blends sm, st, sw

🖍 Write the letters that stand for the first sounds in each word.

 sm

 st

 sw

___

Read the sentences.

🖍 (Circle) the letters that stand for the blends.

1. Stan can be a starfish.

2. Smitty can smile.

3. Swann can swim.

 HOME

Skill: s-Blends

Consonant Digraph sh

Sherry and Shen can share shells.

 Write sh below each picture that begins with the same sound as shells.

 Color the pictures with sh.

_____ _____ _____ _____

_____ _____ _____ _____

_____ _____ _____ _____

_____ _____ _____ _____

HOME

Skill: Initial Consonant Digraph /sh/

Consonant Digraph ch

Cherry and Chase can play chess.

✏️ Write ch below each picture that begins with the same sound as chess.

🖍️ Color the pictures with ch.

_____

   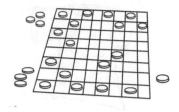

_____

🏠 HOME

Skill: Initial Consonant Digraph /ch/

Consonant Digraph th

Thea and Thatcher can thumb wrestle.

✏️ Write th below each picture that begins with the same sound as thumb.

🖍️ Color the pictures with th.

_____ _____ _____ _____

_____ _____ _____ _____

Skill: Initial Consonant Digraph /th/

Consonant Digraph wh

Whitney can fix
the wheel.

✏️ Write wh below each picture that begins with the
same sound as wheel.

🖍️ Color the pictures with wh.

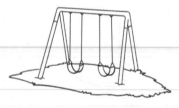

_____   _____   _____   _____

_____   _____   _____   _____

HOME

Skill: Initial Consonant Digraph /hw/ wh

Book 5

They Can

Grace can slide.

Craig can ride a two-wheeler bike.

They can share.

Directions: Help your child tear out this page and the next.
Staple along the cut edge. Have your child read the mini book.

Stan can shampoo Checkers.

Thea can dry Checkers with these white towels.

Grandma can share the drink.

Whitney can share the chicken sandwich.

I can share _____
_____ .

Card Clues

Read how to play on page 64.

Fun and Games

How to play "Card Clues" on page 63:

1. Remove the perforated cards from the book and place them picture side up. Help your child name each picture.

2. Have your child name the first picture on the game board and find the card that has the same target sound. For example, the first picture on the game board is dragon. The matching card is dress.

3. Play until the game board is covered with cards.

4. Mix up the cards and play again.

Use the picture cards to play other games:

• Invite your child to pick a card. Read the picture name. Take turns naming words with the same target sound as the picture. Write the words in pencil. Have your child trace each word with a crayon.

• Pick five picture cards. Have your child name words that rhyme.

• Spread out the cards, picture side up. Have your child find: three cards that begin with the /k/ sound (cat, cup, cake); two cards that end with the /k/ sound (cake, clock); two pairs of cards that rhyme (dress, chess; clock, lock); three cards with the long /ā/ sound (cake, skate, train); one card that ends with the /sh/ sound (fish).

• Select five cards and display the words. Have your child arrange the cards in ABC order.

cat	fish	lock	cup
bed	cake	rope	bike
feet	leaf	paint	roll
boat	cry	child	truck

pretzel	dress	frog	grasshopper
plane	slide	blanket	clock
flag	spoon	snail	star
shell	sweater	chess	thumb